SHIPS OF THE UNION COMPANY

Publisher's Note: The photographs in this book are taken from prints from the collection of the Wellington Harbour Board Maritime Museum. Copyright is held elsewhere for the following: Alexander Turnbull Library, p7 (top); Harraway Collection, Hocken Library, pp7 (lower), 10 (top), 17 (top); G. C. Heron, p25 (top); A. G. Ingram, p36; C. B. Mulholland, pp43, 46 (lower), 47 (lower), 48 (top); *Oamaru Mail*, p42 (lower); USSCo., pp17 (lower), 26 (top), 29 (top), 39 (lower), 45 (lower), 46 (top), 48 (lower).

Cover Photograph: The Picton-Wellington ferry *Tamahine* at Wellington. (WHBMM)

© Crown Copyright Reserved 1989
All rights reserved. No part of this publication may be reproduced by any means, electronic, mechanical, electrostatic photocopying or otherwise, or stored in a retrieval system without the prior permission of the Government Printing Office.

Design: Bill Wieben
Editor: Gavin McLean
Finished Artwork: Production Graphics Rotorua
Typeset in 9/10 pt Century Old Style by Wellington Typesetters Ltd
Printed through Bookprint Consultants, Wellington.

ISBN 0 477 00016 9

INTRODUCTION

The origins of the Union Steam Ship Company of New Zealand Ltd can be traced back to the 1860s when a small group of Dunedin investors led by 'Johnny' Jones formed the Harbour Steam Company to serve gold-rich Otago. After Jones's death in 1869 the company fell into the hands of his ambitious young clerk, James Mills, who steadily amassed more and more power in his hands.

After a false start in 1874, Mills floated his new company the following year. His success was ensured by Scottish shipowner and investor, Peter Denny, who bankrolled the new venture in return for orders for ships. That the backing of Denny and his friends was crucial became obvious in 1876 when metropolitan capital enabled Mills to acquire the fleet of his major rival, the NZ Steam Shipping Company. By the end of the 1880s Union had purchased a host of minor concerns such as the Black Diamond Line, had secured agreement from the NZ-UK lines that they would stay out of the coastal trade and had a stranglehold on the West Coast coal trade.

More crucial expansion took place in 1878 when Union took over the intercolonial (trans-Tasman) services of the Melbourne line, McMeckan, Blackwood & Co. Within four years Denny had consolidated Union's grip on the Tasman with the delivery of seven 1,750-2,000 ton liners, including the revolutionary **Rotomahana** of 1879. Although challenged briefly by James Huddart during the 1890s, the Union Company maintained a near-monopoly of the trade between Australia and NZ until comparatively recent times.

Other growth occurred in the Pacific islands trades, the trans-Pacific (both San Francisco and Vancouver) runs and the Australian coastal routes. Union's 1890 acquisition of the eight ships of the Tasmanian Steam Navigation Co. gave it the control of the lucrative Bass Strait services. From that point the company became as much a household word in Australia as in New Zealand.

By the start of the First World War the company was one of the biggest shipping lines in the world. In terms of tonnage and capital it was bigger than the four largest Australian lines *combined*. Even these figures were misleading because it had been secretly buying into Australian and NZ coastal lines for over a decade. By 1914 it controlled almost all the NZ coastal companies and had substantial shareholdings in Huddart Parker and Wm. Holyman & Sons Ltd.

1917 ended that. Worried about his investments, Mills (a UK resident since 1907) sold the Union Company to British giant P&O. While this brought security, it also brought an end to expansion. The 'Irish County' service on the vital N.Z.-U.K. run, bought from Houlders in 1912, suffered and the company was locked securely into the Pacific routes.

The company diversified into aviation in the 1930s but post-war nationalisation destroyed Union Airways. The company rebuilt its fleet between 1946 and 1960 but steadily lost its remaining bluewater routes (SE Asia and trans-Pacific). By the time that P&O handed control back to Tasman Union Ltd (owned jointly by Australian and NZ interests) its services were confined to Australasia and the Pacific.

The 1970s saw further retrenchment. The company withdrew from the Pacific routes and drastically trimmed its NZ coastal runs. Its share of the crucial trans-Tasman route plunged and quarter-ramp and multi-purpose vessels replaced the remaining conventional ships. At the beginning of 1990 the company operated the 'Seaway' Bass Strait service (**Seaway Hobart** and **Seaway Melbourne**), three trans-

Tasman vessels (***Union Rotorua, Union Rotoiti*** and ***Union Endeavour***), a bulk carrier (***Union Auckland***), a coastal tanker (***Taiko***) and the Chatham Islands supply ship ***Holmdale***. It is also involved ship management, tourism, real estate and other activities.

Author's Note: As the Union Company has owned more than 350 ships, this selection can do more than provide a representative sampling. Readers requiring a more detailed view of the company and its fleet are advised to consult ***Union Fleet*** by Ian Farquhar (N.Z. Ship & Marine Society, Wellington 1968 and 1976), ***Glamour Ships of the Union Steam Ship Company*** by Jack Churchouse (Millwood Press, Wellington, 1981), ***Steamships*** by D. F. Gardiner and J. E. Hobbs (Millwood Press/ NZ Ship & Marine Society, 1982) and ***The Line That Dared***, edited by Gordon McLauchlan (Four Star Press, Auckland, 1987).

The Union Company started with five small steam coasters, the **Maori** (above, 174 tons, 1875-84 and 1888-1902), **Beautiful Star** (below, 177 tons 1875-99), **Bruce** (335 tons) and the new **Hawea** and **Taupo**.

The new, highly efficient compound engines of the **Hawea** (above, 721 tons, 1875-88) made her an exceptional ship for her day.

The **Taranaki** (below, 415 tons, 1876-78) was one of four ships taken over in 1876 from Union's principal competitor, the NZ Steam Shipping Co. She ran ashore near Tauranga on 29 November 1888.

The company snapped up several smaller shipping companies during the late 1870s. One ship acquired this way was the Oamaru & Dunedin Steam Co.'s **Waitaki** *(above, 412 tons, 1879-83).*

The **Penguin** *(below, 749 tons, 1879-1909) came from British owners.*

Although the **Wakatipu** had run in the intercolonial (trans-Tasman) trade under 'friendly' owners, the company first entered the run in its own right with the acquisition of McMeckan, Blackwood & Co.'s four ships, of which the **Ringarooma** *(1,096 tons, 1878-1901)* was the best.

The **Te Anau** *(1,652 tons, 1879-1924)* was one of the first built for the new service. Her master's cabin is preserved in the Wellington Harbour Board Maritime Museum.

The intercolonial liner **Rotomahana** *(1,797 tons, 1879-1925) was a ship of superlatives. The first merchant ship to be built of mild steel and the first fitted with bilge keels, she made a tremendous impact on the new service. She finished up on the Bass Strait run.*

9

*Between 1882 and 1883 the Union Company built five new 2,000 ton liners for the intercolonial routes: the **Manapouri** (above, 1,783 tons, 1882-1915), **Wairarapa** (below, 1,786 tons, 1882-94), **Hauroto** (1,988 tons, 1882-1915), **Tarawera** (2,003 tons 1882-1927) and **Waihora** (2,003 tons, 1883).*

*Seen here later in her career, the **Tarawera** (1882-1927), the company's first ship to exceed 2,000 tons, ended up on the NZ coast as a cargo vessel.*

*The **Mararoa** (2,466 tons, 1885-1931) made a big name for herself in the trans-Pacific, intercolonial and Lyttleton-Wellington runs.*

During the 1880s the company also built up its coastal fleet. The **Takapuna** *(above, 930 tons, 1883-1924) ran a high speed service between Lyttelton and Onehunga; she was expensive and unsuccessful. More typical of acquisitions of the period was the collier* **Kawatiri** *(below, 453 tons 1887-1907), one of three purchased from the Westport Coal Co. in 1887.*

Typical of the multi-purpose cargo vessels added to the fleet during the 1880s and 1890s were the second **Taupo** *(above, 737 tons, 1884-1900), pictured here in Avatiu Harbour, Rarotonga, and the second* **Wanaka** *(below, 2,425 tons, 1897-1927).*

One of the company's major coups was its purchase — against the opposition of Australian competitor Huddart Parker Ltd — of the Tasmanian Steam Navigation Company in 1891. This gave it the lion's share of the lucrative Bass Strait services. The eight ships in this deal included the **Talune** (above, 1,991 tons, 1891-1925) and the **Flora** (below, 1,283 tons, 1891-1927).

*Between 1898 and 1911 the company replaced its earlier trans-Tasman liners with a series of six modern ships. The **Moeraki** (above, 4,392 tons, 1902-33) and **Manuka** (below, 4,505 tons, 1903-29) were half-sisters.*

*The next intercolonial liner, the **Maheno** (above, 5,282 tons, 1905-35) was one of the first large merchant ships to be powered by turbines. Unfortunately they were not successful and the ship had to be re-engined. The **Marama** (below, 6,437 tons, 1907-37) was more conventional and reliable; she served a variety of routes.*

As the Denny yard was a world leader in the development of the marine turbine engine, it was only natural that the Union Company would test this new system. Its Melbourne-Launceston ferry **Loongana** *(above, 2,448 tons, 1905-22) was the world's first turbine-powered deep sea merchant vessel. The Lyttelton-Wellington ferry* **Maori** *(below, 3,399 tons 1907-46) was another very successful pioneer.*

*The company's growing fleet required the use of a few harbour tugs. The **Natone**, although Australian-built, (above, 73 tons, 1900-47) spent virtually all her career on Wellington Harbour, towing oil barges and tending coal hulks. The **Terawhiti** (below, 260 tons, 1907-47), also based at Wellington, was a powerful deep-sea salvage tug.*

The **Wairuna** (above, 3,947 tons, 1904-17) served mainly on the trans-Pacific runs until sunk by the German raider **Wolf** in June 1917.

The **Kotuku** (below, 1,054 tons, 1900-12) also had a short life, going ashore at Greymouth in May 1912.

*In the years leading up to the First World War, the company revamped its trans-Pacific services with the liners **Makura** (above, 8,075 tons, 1908-36) and **Niagara** (below, 13,415 tons, 1913-31). The **Niagara**, the first British liner to burn oil fuel, served with associate venture Canadian Australasian Line Ltd (jointly owned with CPR) between 1931 and 1940.*

*In 1912 the company finally obtained a foothold in the massive NZ-UK trade with the purchase of the Houlder Bros.' four ship 'Irish County' service. Two ships built especially for the run were the **Leitrim** (above, 9,540 tons, 1916-29) and the stately **Armagh** (below, 12,269 tons, 1917-23).*

In 1924 Union took delivery of its long-awaited consort to the **Niagara**, the **Aorangi** (above, 17,491 tons, 1924-31). The largest motor vessel in the world when built, the **Aorangi** served with associate company Australasian Line Ltd until 1953. The smaller Picton-Wellington ferry **Tamahine** (below, 1,989 tons, 1925-62) sailed with her perpetual list until replaced by the modern Cook Strait road/rail ferries.

Three of the passenger ships added to the fleet during the 1930s: the trans-Tasman liner **Monowai** *(previous page, 10,852 tons, 1930-60), a former P&O ship, the Lyttelton-Wellington ferry* **Rangatira** *(above, 6,152 tons) and the Pacific trader* **Matua** *(below, 4,166 tons, 1936-68).*

*Two 1920s freighters. The **Poolta** (above, 1,675 tons, 1925-52) was acquired from the Tasmanian government in 1925. The **Kaimiro** (below, 2,562 tons, 1929-54) was one of a pair (the other being the **Karepo** [2,563 tons, 1929-54]) of impressive engines-aft colliers built by Cammell Laird & Co. Ltd at the start of the depression.*

*During the 1930s Union added a number of smaller modern ships to its fleet. Two of the more outstanding were the **Karu** (above, 1,044 tons 1935-64) and the **Kauri** (below, 2,361 tons, 1936-62). Like so many Union Company ships of the period, they were built by A. Stephen & Sons Ltd of Glasgow.*

*The **Kakapo** (above, 2,498 tons, 1937-60) survived the Second World War, as did the war-built **Kaimanawa** (below, shown armed, 2,577 tons, 1944-66).*

*In 1946-47 the company re-established its coastal services with the modified Admiralty supply ships **Kanna** (above, 925 tons, 1946-67) and **Katui** (925 tons, 1946-67) and the German war prize **Kamo** (below, 1,450 tons, 1947-58). As the **Gaarden**, the **Kamo** had been built as a special supply vessel for the battleship **Tirpitz**.*

*Although overshadowed by the **Rangatira**, the Lyttelton-Wellington ferry **Hinemoa** (6,911 tons, 1946-67) was a significant ship in her own right. Based on the general design of the **Rangatira**, she was the first major post-war British passenger vessel. She ended her days as the Tasmanian accommodation vessel **George H. Evans**.*

The Union Company turned to war-built standard designs to rebuild its deep water services. In 1947-48 it acquired the **Wairata** (5,255 tons 1947-67) and **Wairimu** (6,796 tons, 1948-66). They were U.S. C2-type freighters and ran to India and SE Asia.

The **Waitemata** (below, 7,364 tons, 1946-67), was a Canadian-built vessel modified on the stocks to a Union design.

The **Waikawa** (above 7,185 tons, 1946-59) and **Wairuna** (below 7,212 tons, 1946-60), sisters to the **Waitemata**, featured the class's original simple superstructure. The five standard ships maintained the company's North American cargo service until the mid 1960s.

Two of the few post-war passenger vessels were the Islands trader **Tofua** *(above, 5,299 tons, 1951-73) and the Lyttelton-Wellington ferry* **Maori** *(below 8,303 tons, 1953-74).*

The post-war reconstruction programme centred around the 'slow greens', the 5,000 dwt trans-Tasman freighters. The **Komata** *(above, 3,543 tons, 1947-67) and the* **Waimate** *(below, 3,506 tons, 1951-72), while slightly different (the* **Waimate** *featuring 'tween decks), belonged to the first 'AE' group. (USSCo.)*

The 'AC' group of smaller 3,000 dwt ships included the **Kaitawa** *(above, 2,485 tons, 1949-66) and the* **Kokiri** *(below, 2,470 tons, 1951-68). The* **Kaitawa** *went down with all hands off the northern tip of NZ on 23 May 1966. The* **Kokiri**'s *light cargo gear made her unique.*

*Two of the smaller post-war freighters were the **Navua** (above, 1,952 tons, 1955-71) and the **Konui** (below, 1,285 tons, 1949-69). The **Navua**, built for the Pacific trade, spent most of her career with a white hull although this did not save her from the indignity of having to load dirty coal cargoes from time to time!*

The **Kaitoa** (above, 2,584 tons, 1956-71) and the **Konini** (below, 2,007 tons, 1957-71) were typical Henry Robb Ltd products. The Kaitoa was an 'AC' modification for the general cargo trade.

The **Tarawera** (above, 2,013 tons, 1958-74) was the company's first non-British or non-Australasian new building. She was built by Hong Kong's Taikoo Dockyard & Eng. Co. Ltd as a small refrigerated cargo carrier.

The **Kaimiro** (below, 3,722 tons, 1956-75) was one of a six ship batch of 'AE' class trans-Tasman freighters.

The 'AE' class formed the backbone of the trans-Tasman trade and served until replaced by the new ro-ros in 1975. The **Koranui** (above, 3,722 tons, 1956-75) was a standard ship but the **Waikare** (below, 3,839 tons, 1958-750 was a 'tween decks variant incorporating refrigerated space.

One of the smaller ships for the Australian trades was the **Pateena** (above, 2,099 tons, 1958-75).

The last conventional ship built for Australian service was the specialist zinc concentrates carrier **Risdon** (below, 4,125 tons, 1959-75). Built by Alec Stephen & Sons Ltd, she traded between Port Pirie and Risdon.

The **Poolta** (2,085 tons, 1959-75) was one of the last conventional ships built for the Tasmanian trade. The unit load revolution was near at hand and in 1968 the company sent her to Hong Kong's Taikoo Dockyard where a 20 metre section was added and deck cranes replaced her derricks. Sold in 1975, the **Poolta** was still trading between N.Z. and the Pacific Islands in 1988.

*In 1964 after many years' planning, the Union Company introduced its first unit load vessels, the **Seaway Queen** (2,961 tons, 1964-75) and **Seaway King** (2,961 tons, 1964-76). Hybrid ships, they handled cargo via a combination of deck cranes and a stern door. They ran on the Melbourne-Hobart and Sydney-Hobart routes until replaced by a new generation of 'Seaway' ships in 1975-76.*

The ro-ro ships were supplemented by new 'crane ships' in which high-speed deck cranes replaced conventional derricks. The **Karetu** (3,222 tons, 1964-80), pictured above on trials and below at Oamaru, and the **Karepo** (3,222 tons, 1964-78) were fine-looking vessels with excellent crew accommodation.

*The other crane ships were the 'N' class, built in two batches, the **Ngakuta** (above, 4,576 tons, 1962-83) and **Ngatoro** (4,576 tons, 1962-76) and the **Ngahere** (4,575 tons, 1966-87) and **Ngapara** (below 4,575 tons, 1966-86). Built primarily for carrying forest products across the Tasman, they were extremely successful. The **Ngahere** later gained fame as NZ's 'Ship of Hope' famine relief ship to Ethiopia.*

*The Lyttelton-Wellington steamer express service went ro-ro in the mid 1960s with the conversion of the **Maori** and the construction of the **Wahine** (8,944 tons, 1966-68). The **Wahine**, pictured above, sank with the loss of 51 lives in Wellington Harbour on 10 April 1968. Her replacement, the **Rangatira** (below, 9,387 tons, 1972-76) was owned by a P&O subsidiary and chartered to the Union Company.*

With the striking-looking **Hawea** (above, 2,268 tons, 1967-76) and **Wanaka** (below, 2,769 tons, 1970-76) the Union Company attempted to shore up its beleaguered NZ coastal cargo services. The **Wanaka** could always be distinguished by her larger after deckhouse and the absence of the deck crane.

The strategic trans-Tasman run 'went ro-ro' in 1969 with the delivery of the **Maheno** (above, 4,510 tons, 1969-75) and **Marama** (4,510 tons, 1969-76 and 1981-85). Cargo was loaded through the stern door on specially-designed 'Seafreighters'.

The expensive new ro-ro ships were supplemented by modern bulk carriers. The **Union New Zealand** (above, 3,166 tons, 1972) was one of three small 'Camit' type mini-bulkers chartered in 1972-73.

*The cargo liner **Union Aotearoa** (below, 6,732 tons, 1973), also chartered, reopened the SE Asian route for the company before being diverted to the Tasman.*

*To cope with the burgeoning trans-Tasman traffic, the company bought or chartered a number of ro-ro vessels during the early 1970s. One charter vessel was the **Union Sydney** (below, 4,752 tons, 1974).*

In 1976-77 the company took delivery of two massive quarter ramp vessels, the gas-turbine powered **Union Rotorua** *(23,971 tons, 1977-)* and **Union Rotoiti** *(23,962 tons, 1976-)*. The **Union Rotoiti** has since been re-engined with diesels. Supplemented by the multi-purpose ship **Union Endeavour** and the bulk carrier **Union Auckland** they form the mainstay of the company's trans-Tasman 'bridge'.